Ronald Reagan

A Ronald Reagan Biography

Anna Revell

Copyright © 2017.

All rights reserved. No part of this publication may be reproduced, distributed, or transmitted in any form or by any means, including photocopying, recording, or other electronic or mechanical methods, without the prior written permission of the publisher, except in the case of brief quotations embodied in critical reviews and certain other noncommercial uses permitted by copyright law.

This book is intended for informational and entertainment purposes only. The publisher limits all liability arising from this work to the fullest extent of the law.

Table of Contents

The Enduring Romance of Ronald Reagan

Early Life

The Call of Tinseltown

Hollywood Playboy

A Love Story for the Ages

Political Theater

Defection and Scandal

'A Rendezvous with Destiny…'

The Road to the White House

Ronald Reagan's Leading Role: President of the United States

'Morning Again in America'

The Iran-Contra Affair

Exit Stage Left

The Enduring Romance of Ronald Reagan

Ronald Reagan made his living as a peddler of dreams.

In Hollywood, which sits on the City of (Broken or Otherwise) Dreams, he was a successful actor listed in more than 80 projects over the span of a long career from 1937 to 1965. Though he was never quite the leading man, his films would cultivate the tough, folksy cowboy image and its associate visions of a mythic, frontier America, that would help him succeed in politics. In Hollywood, he would also hone the skills that would one day land him the title of The Great Communicator - able to hold a room, convey a vision, and make a conversion.

Concurrent to his acting work, Reagan was spokesman for General Electric for eight years, from 1954 to 1962. In this capacity, he sold another dream – science and progress – but also began to acquire different dreams of his own. His work for General Electric took him across the country on tours as a goodwill ambassador, visiting GE factories and their communities, putting him in the path to mingle with businessmen and workers, and placing him within reach and easy recall of the American public. Looking back now, it was a dress rehearsal for the physical demands of a political career. But it wasn't just good practice for a glad-handing pol. Along the way, he built the cornerstones of an emerging political philosophy.

As a politician, he advocated a particular vision of America, a vision that would carry him into the highest office of the land – President of the United States. It was a vision that would be held dreamily forever afterwards by many in the Republican Party: an America of free enterprise, unencumbered by federal government overreach, unburdened by excessive taxation, the home of individual liberty and achievement. Ronald Reagan, as political tough guy and cowboy, became the champion and embodiment of this vision.

Whether or not one agreed with his overarching vision, Reagan was, at the very least, an optimist, a party unifier, an electable conservative with broad appeal. He was a popular president the likes of which many would hope to see again.

So much is the yearning of many American voters for someone to take over that mantle, that channeling Ronald Reagan had become an essential part of the ambitious Republican politician's campaign playbook. In January 2017, President Donald Trump tweeted an old photo of himself shaking hands with President Ronald Reagan as the latter's First Lady, Nancy, looked on with a small smile. Never mind that it was hardly a ringing endorsement; they were never friends, and Reagan had even misspelled his own name in signing the photo addressed to the then-real estate mogul. Association and imagery were enough for Trump. Indeed, invocations of Ronald Reagan and attempts to bask in the halo of the deified Republican, wouldn't end there.

Senator John McCain, who ran for President against Barack Obama under the Republican banner in the historic elections of 2008, referred to himself as a Reagan Republican. Like Trump, he would spread around a photo of himself with the late President (unlike Trump, however, he and Nancy Reagan were longtime friends). It is especially notable that his announcement of running for the highest office in the land came with many mentions of Ronald Reagan.

House Speaker Paul Ryan wrote about "the Gipper" in his book, *The Way Forward: Renewing the American Idea*, remembering him for being an exceptional politician and praising his determination to get the country back on the right path. Arkansas Governor Mike Huckabee's *A Simple Government* sang praises for Reagan's economic management. Texas Governor Rick Perry also had Reagan in mind in *Fed Up!: Our Fight to Save America from Washington*, where he remarked on the former President as an inspiration.

The path to success seemed clear – if you wanted the support of a fervent, loyal base, you had to woo them by lionizing the Republican Party's most enduring – and endearing – figure.

The base has cause to continually long for the days of Reagan, and yearn for the resurgence of any politician reminiscent of him. But like all romantic figures, like all historical myths, like the heroes he himself has portrayed on screen – how Reagan is currently perceived by many is a mix of the real and the idealized or sometimes even imagined. This, after all, is the essence of a romance; reality mixed in longing.

His image of a tough guy, cowboy Hollywood star? Well, he wasn't a very good actor and most of his roles were in the supporting capacity. His body of work in the industry would be best remembered by two roles in which he played an amputee (in *King's Row*, 1942), and an ill, dying man (in *Knute Rockne - All American*, 1940). He also wasn't much of a macho man before his wife Nancy, who, while she openly adored him, reportedly was also masterful in managing him. His first wife, an acclaimed actress, allegedly left him out of boredom and/or because her career had overtaken his. Previous girlfriends have said he was attractive, but unexciting. He was indeed attractive; athletic with an impressive figure.

He would even walk into the hospital on his own power after a gunshot wound to the chest. But he had myopia bad enough to keep him from fighting in World War II, and in the 1980s he was open about his hearing problems.

His charisma and easy charm? This did not appear to have translated in his personal life, especially when one realizes he cherished his alone time, had no interest in casual or personal talk with most people, and so never really had a lot of true friends over his life (except for wife Nancy). He also wouldn't have a controversy-free relationship with members of his own family. His children, Patti (by Nancy) and Michael (adopted from his first marriage), would write books with some unflattering tales of growing up as a Reagan. Among them, Patti's account of how sometimes, it seemed as if Ronald needed to be reminded of who his children were. Michael would share a tale about how he was told he was excluded from Ronald and Nancy's will.

His vision of a smaller government with cuts to spending? They didn't quite pan out. From the time he was in office in 1981 to when he stepped down in 1989, total federal government employment rose – including in the Executive branch. When he came into office, the budget had $599 billion in revenues, $678 billion in spending, and a $79 billion deficit. When he left? It was at $909 billion, about $1.1 trillion, and $155 billion, respectively. Federal spending grew too, even adjusted for inflation.

As for his economic achievements, they may as well be debated to kingdom come. Regarding his efforts at deregulation, some critics argue that his policies helped usher in a massive financial crisis that eventually resulted in a taxpayer-funded government bailout in 1991 – hardly the ideal illustration of the benefits of a free market. His policies have also been partially blamed for America's most recent economic crisis in 2008.

His record on tax cuts was mixed too. 1981 saw one of the largest tax cuts ever… except he followed it up with the largest peacetime tax increase, The Tax Equity and Fiscal Responsibility Act of 1982. His succeeding years in office also had additional gas levies, a corporate tax increase and a rise in payroll taxes.

His hawkish stance in international affairs? Well he actually showed more nuance, flexibility and restraint. Sure, he built up the military. But he also had productive exchanges with the Soviet Union – moves that would help usher in the end of the Cold War. He also wasn't particularly tough on terrorism. He was mostly unwilling to retaliate militarily, if it meant operations could endanger civilians. He also signed the United Nations Convention Against Torture in 1988.

His image as a defender of freedom in America and abroad wasn't very straightforward either. Sure, the fall of the Soviet Union in a sense emancipated parts of Eastern Europe. But in Africa, Asia and Latin America, he had to make tough tradeoffs between supporting oppressive governments and the Marxist threat that he considered to be such a priority, so he actually aided or failed to contest the former so as not to risk the latter.

As for his rehabilitation of the image of the office of the President? Awesome, he was certainly well-liked, especially after Vietnam-burdened Lyndon B. Johnson, Watergate-ousted Richard Nixon, uninspiring Gerald Ford and gloomy Jimmy Carter. But the Iran-Contra affair showed he was not immune to questionable and secretive acts in office. The Iran-Contra affair also exposed his lack of control and knowledge of the workings of some of his appointees.

He wasn't even as well-loved as today's devout Reaganites like to imagine and portray. Sure, he is a popular President among the upper echelons of his peers with the likes of the adored JFK and irrepressible Bill Clinton, but over his eight years in office, his approval ratings according to Gallup averaged at 53%, with peaks and valleys seemingly negating each other.

Speaking of public image, Ronald Reagan is considered a champion of the right-wing and he is certainly a lightning rod of today's Republican ambitions. But overall, he seemed less of a hard-liner on conservative ideas but more of a pragmatic conservative. He famously worked productively with the Soviet Union and Gorbachev yes, so how hard is it to believe and accept that he also managed to work with Democrats at home to achieve his objectives? He was even able to attain cross-party and independent votes in both his runs for President. He was open to make compromises if it meant partial wins.

History, for the most part, has been kind to Ronald Reagan. But it would be a grave injustice if we did not pull back the curtains, and expose the man behind the myth. Because whatever myth we would eventually attach to his legend, the bare facts still had the makings of a great man. There is no need to whitewash his complexity to see his greatness. The Gipper is tough enough to handle it.

Ronald Reagan, whether one agreed with his politics or not, whether one believed he had achieved the objectives of the vision he espoused or not - was still someone who pulled himself up from incarnation to incarnation, to reach impossible dreams both Hollywood and political. He still ushered in an end to the Cold War, with the American way of life squarely on top. He still had a winning vision that remains resonant to many in the country he loved. He still sits upon the bar that most Republican politicians hope to attain and surpass. He still has a voice and input in the politics of our day. He still has wide-ranging impacts for American political life, long after his death. He is still a lightning rod for dreams.

It would be an injustice not to look at him with a critical eye, because if he was just a man - with real flaws, real difficulties, and one who had to make real, hard decisions – then it would have made his achievements all the greater.

To simply live with the romanticized image and not examine the reality of Ronald Reagan would also be unjust to his message of individual ability and potential for greatness. Because if we detach him from our flawed ordinariness, then how can we truly find and replicate the best parts of him in ourselves? How can we live by that image he has championed, of Americans as free individuals with self-determination and an ability to make his country truly great?

And so let us pull back the curtains. Let us go behind the scenes. Let us de-mystify Ronald Reagan and unpack the romance he has spun around American political life and in so doing – create the possibility of finding him in ourselves.

Early Life

Ronald Wilson Reagan was born to Jack and Nelle Reagan, on the 6th of February, 1911. He was born in an apartment above a general store in Tampico, Illinois. It wouldn't be home for very long, as they would settle in Dixon by 1920. The man who would become a shining beacon of light for the Republican Party was the child of Democrat parents. Jack Reagan, who had been a salesman, eventually became a local director for Franklin D. Roosevelt's Works Progress Administration, which was a federal agency established to help unemployed Americans find work. Ronald's older brother Neil also worked there. As for their mother Nelle, she was active in her church, the Disciples of Christ, and was relentless in doing compassionate work for prisoners, the poor, and the ill. She was just as considerate in her own home; Jack was an alcoholic. Indeed, some of the future President's childhood memories included dragging his unconscious father home. But Nelle looked upon Jack's alcoholism as a disease and steered their children toward that same understanding. Ronald always had great things to say about his mother, who had also worked as a seamstress and salesclerk to help the family. She would also be instrumental in his passion for performing; when they were younger, she involved them in drama performances.

Ronald attended Dixon High School until 1928. There, he was active in the arts, sports and student government. He was in the basketball and football teams, he was president of the student body, a writer for the yearbook, and appeared in plays. In the summers, he worked as a lifeguard – with a reported 77 saves.

He was just as active in college, attending Eureka College in Illinois from 1928 to 1932. He attended on a partial football scholarship and had to work to cover other education costs, as well as to send funds for his family. He washed dishes at a girl's dormitory as well as at his own fraternity, Tau Kappa Epsilon. He was also a lifeguard and a swimming coach.

He wasn't a particularly gifted student, finishing with an unimpressive average of "C" upon graduation. But what he lacked in one aspect of student life, he excelled at in others. In sports, he was involved in teams for swimming and again, football. He still wrote, this time for the school paper. He was in debate and drama, and was also student council president. His gift for mixing communication and governance would manifest itself very early in his college life; as a freshman, he delivered a stirring address at a student strike protesting class suspensions due to the financial constraints of the Great Depression.

The Call of Tinseltown

It seemed like anywhere he went, Ronald Reagan had the makings of a star.

After graduation, he found work as a radio sportscaster in Davenport, Iowa. He did not have a lot of experience, but he had a broadcaster's silky, baritone voice and he proved to be a quick study. He became staff announcer, and soon made the move to Des Moines, Iowa, working for an NBC radio outlet. But radio could only hold him for so long; he had an outsize personality and matinee idol looks. He was tall at six-feet and one inch. His brown hair was wavy, he had blue eyes and a winning smile. Ronald Reagan was hard to miss, plus he had experience on the stage. In 1937, he was on assignment to cover the Chicago Cubs' training in California. He was also there to meet with an agent, and change the course of his life.

A screen test with Warner Brothers would seal the deal, and kick start a career in the entertainment industry that would find him in 52 Hollywood films from 1937 to 1957. For Ronald Reagan, Hollywood dreams that were elusive to many seemingly came in a cinch. On June 1st 1937, he closed a Warner Brother Contract. Four months later, *Love Is on the Air* was released – where the tailor-made role had him playing Andy McCaine, a radio commentator.

He continued working, eventually finding his most memorable role in 1940, playing George Gipp in *Knute Rockne - All American*. Gipp was a gifted Notre Dame halfback who had a promising career ahead of him, steered along by Coach Rockne until he was stricken down by illness in his prime. His deathbed request – "*… someday when the team is up against it, when the breaks are beatin' the boys, ask 'em to go in there with all they've got and win just one for the Gipper.*" It was an iconic scene, well-written and well-acted, an instant movie classic. The role would only give Reagan 15 minutes of screen time, but he would carry the nickname, "The Gipper" for a lifetime, because the unforgettable line would become a rallying cry his political devotees would always stay true to.

Reagan's time in Hollywood would also be memorable for outputs like 1942's *King's Row*, where he played Drake McHugh, a small town rake who made the mistake of going after the doctor's daughter. Following an accident, the physician needlessly amputated his legs, prompting him to cry the classic line, *"Where's the rest of me?"* Reagan was great in the film, and he would go on to use the memorable, despairing question as the title of his 1965 autobiography.

Ronald Reagan found a lucrative place in Hollywood, playing leads in B-movies and supporting roles in more prominent productions. In his supporting capacity, he often appeared as the guy who loses the girl to the lead or the guy who is the best friend of the lead. "*I was the Errol Flynn of the B-pictures,*" the self-aware President would say years later, of his constant part in low-budget films that made big-money for the studios. Indeed, he would be supporting the top-billing, swashbuckling star, Errol Flynn, in 1940's *Santa Fe Trail* and 1942's *Desperate Journey*. The latter was Reagan's last role prior to joining World War II. He had been in the U.S. Army Cavalry Reserve for almost a decade by that time, but during the war itself, he was in a sense, in the "supporting role" too. Poor eyesight kept him stateside, where he worked making propaganda films for the armed forces' First Motion Picture

Unit. In this capacity, he was the voice of training films, and appeared in patriotic, objective-oriented projects for the war effort. 1943's *Rear Gunner*, for example, was made to address a shortage of gunners in the Air Corps. That same year, he was part of the musical, *This is the Army*, which raised millions of funds for charities during the war.

He was definitely a man in uniform, even if it was primarily in the movies. Few Presidents could match the frequency by which Ronald Reagan must have been seen by the public in some sort of distinguished uniform; for example in the two films with Errol Flynn listed above, his work during the war, and a slew of other projects including *Sergeant Murphy* (1938), *The Voice of the Turtle* (1947) and *The Hasty Heart* (1949).

He wasn't particularly gifted as an actor, and the hoped-for performance Oscar by many in his field would not be in the cards for the future-POTUS. Nevertheless, his time as an actor formed the public perception of him as a man in uniform. It would also be useful in cultivating his folk hero, cowboy image. Like many actors of his generation, Reagan appeared in a number of Westerns around the 1950s, like *Tennessee's Partner* (1955) and *Cattle Queens of Montana* (1954). But it wasn't all show; he had a particular love of horses, did his own riding stunts and owned a ranch. The cowboy image, just like the Gipper nickname, would follow him into politics.

Because Reagan was generally unimposing on screen, he was often eclipsed by his female co-stars. In *Dark Victory* (1939), he shared the screen with the ever-compelling Bette Davis. In *John Loves Mary* (1949) and *The Hasty Heart* (1949), Patricia Neal was a scene-stealer. In *Storm Warning* (1951), it was Ginger Rogers and Doris Day. In real life too, it was his first wife, Jane Wyman, getting all the accolades. She would win an Oscar in 1949 for her role in *Johnny Belinda*.

Hollywood Playboy

In Hollywood, Ronald Reagan acquired the image of best friend, man in uniform and cowboy. Here he also honed the communication skills that would make him a formidable force in politics. But the most important thing he found in Hollywood was probably love – twice!

His first wife was born Sarah Jane Mayfield on the 5th of January 1917 (some say 1914) in

Missouri. Her parents divorced in 1921 and her father died the following year. In 1928 she moved to California and tried for the first time to find her place in films, but would return to Missouri just two years later. She attended university and became a radio singer, which gave her a better path to stardom. Eventually under the name Jane Wyman, she broke into Hollywood in 1935 with her first film, the musical, *King of Burlesque*. She was a chorus dancer. By 1936, however, she became a contract player for Warner Bros., and debuted as an actress for a small part in *Gold Diggers* (1937).

Like the man who would one day be her husband, Jane Wyman was a B-movie actress and supporting player in larger films. But by 1945, she would gain more attention as a serious actress of considerable talent, when she played an alcoholic's girlfriend in Billy Wilder's *The Lost Weekend*. More meaty parts would follow, and would not escape the notice of the Academy Awards. She was nominated for her performance in *The Yearling* (1946) opposite Gregory Peck; and would win the Best Actress award for *Johnny Belinda* (1948), where she played a raped deaf-mute girl. Not only did she not speak dialogue, she was a 34-year-old playing a teenager. She would be eyed for an Oscar several more times – in 1951's *Blue Veil* and 1954's *Magnificent Obsession*. She picked up a reputation as "one-take Wyman" for her professionalism and skill. She continued to do films until 1969, and also found success in television as a host and drama actress.

She was successful in her career, but less so in love. In 1933, at only 16 years of age, she was married to one Ernest Eugene Wyman but only for two years. A couple of years later, in 1937, she married again, to one Myron Futterman, a clothing manufacturer. They divorced in 1938. Third time still wasn't the charm, however…

In 1938 she met the up-and-coming Ronald Reagan when they shared the screen for *Brother Rat*. They married in 1940 and was packaged to look like the ideal young couple. Their union gave them a baby girl in 1941, whom they named Maureen. She would be followed by an adopted son, Michael in 1945. The couple lost who would have been their third child, a daughter born premature in 1947. Reagan and Wyman divorced shortly afterwards, in 1948.

Wyman would find love again in 1952 with studio music director Fred Karger, whom she would divorce, remarry, and divorce again by 1965. Wyman passed away in 2007 at the age of 90, at home in California.

Being the ex-wife of the first (and for a long time, until Donald Trump came into office, the only) divorced U.S. President couldn't have been easy. Wyman was still a prominent figure in the industry when Reagan came into the White House in the 1980s; she was Angela Channing, tyrannical family matriarch in the hit CBS drama, *Falcon Crest*. But she kept a steely, graceful silence about the failed relationship and so did the President. Eight years the couple spent together – but President Reagan reportedly only wrote out a couple of short sentences about his first wife in his memoirs. Such secrecy made the relationship even more intriguing, and it was a subject in a number of books that would later come out about Ronald Reagan's love life.

By some accounts, Jane and Ronald started seeing each other while she was still Mrs. Myron Futterman. Reagan was reportedly wary of adultery, but pursued the romance once assured the marriage was already falling apart. Their own marriage would find its own crumbling way to a divorce by 1948, but their eight years together created a great deal of publicity depicting them as the ideal couple, especially as they started a family. The divorce could have been caused by a number of factors, but among those that have been suggested by biographers include Wyman getting bored of her husband, especially as her career really began to soar following all the recognition she was finally getting from the Academy Awards. His, on the other hand, was languishing post-war. Others say they may have had differences in opinion relating to having more children, which would have taken a toll on her career. By other theories, she found he was getting too involved with the affairs of the Screen Actors Guild – where he would have his first taste of big-time politics in its board and eventually as its president. Either way, the end of his first marriage was reportedly devastating to the future POTUS, who was rumored to alternate between charming a bevy of women, and being depressed by his divorce.

Though nothing is verified, the list of women allegedly charmed by the future POTUS in his Hollywood years is impressive –

counting such iconic beauties and legends as Ava Gardner, Betty Grable, Doris Day, Lana Turner, and possibly even Marilyn Monroe herself. Even if he didn't win over these fine ladies in particular, however, it is still widely-believed that he had a magic touch with women. Co-star Virginia Mayo, with whom he starred in a couple of films, revealed in a magazine interview in the 1980s that Reagan had a number of girlfriends dropping by the set.

It is one lesser-known, B-movie actress named Nancy Davis, however, who would not only win the Gipper's heart and keep it, she would also propel him into one of the hardest roles to win and the toughest parts to play: that of Leader of the Free World, the President of the United States of America.

A Love Story for the Ages

Nancy Reagan, born the 6th of July 1921, was, like many First Ladies of the United States, born in New York. She was born under the name Anne Frances Robbins, only child to Edith Luckett Robins and Kenneth Robbins. Edith was an actress and Kenneth, a salesman. Kenneth and Edith divorced in 1928 and Anne –nicknamed "Nancy" in her youth – would be raised by her aunt and uncle in Bethesda, Maryland. She attended Sidwell Friends School there from 1925-1928. She would still see her mother though, especially when Edith was in New York for her theater career.

Edith would find love again after Kenneth, in the form of Chicago-based neurosurgeon, Loyal Davis. They married in 1929, and

Nancy was eventually legally adopted by Loyal in the 1930s. Davis was prominent in his field, and as his daughter, Nancy had the advantages associated with his privileged lifestyle. Her education included Girls' Latin School in Chicago (1929 - 1939), and eventually, a Bachelor of Arts degree with Smith College in Northampton, Massachusetts (1939 – 1943), where she took up drama. Loyal Davis wasn't just influential in Nancy's life; the staunch conservative would also reportedly have an impact in changing the views of Nancy's husband, Ronald Reagan, with whom he actively shared political views. But that would come later, in the 1950s.

In 1943, after graduation, Nancy Davis first entered the workforce as a sales clerk in Marshall Fields Department Store, and then as a nurse's aide, both in Chicago. But with some help from her mother's connections, she was able to begin breaking into the entertainment industry. Her debut was a nonspeaking part in a touring production of the play, *Ramshackle Inn*, which eventually brought her to New York. In Broadway, she secured a small role in the 1946 Yul Brenner and Mary Martin starrer, *Lute Song*.

1949 would find her across the country in Hollywood, with a seven-year contract with Metro Goldwyn Mayer. She wasn't quite the hit actress, but she did have a number of projects under her belt, among them *The Doctor and the Girl* (1949) *East Side, West Side* (1949) and *Night into Morning* (1951). She wasn't known to be a great actress, but she also had a handicap early in her life in Tinseltown – "Nancy Davis" was supposedly on the Hollywood blacklist, an actress suspected of being a sympathizer to communists. It was at the time, a potential career killer. The woman on the list was actually an actress of the same name, rather than the Nancy Davis and future FLOTUS that we know. Either way, the incident might have killed her shot at potential parts, but it sure opened up a whole new world for the young actress, because it compelled her to get in touch with the President of the Screen Actors Guild to see if he could assist in her predicament. At the time, that role was played by none other than Ronald Reagan, an anti-Communist (he even became an FBI informant) who enforced the industry's stance against it, but was also reasonable about the bans embroiling innocent artists.

By most accounts, sparks flew right away and the attraction was mutual and immediate. They met over dinner, and that "date" reportedly ended at 3 in the morning, with promises of more to come – including a date for the very next day.

The attraction was quick, but they opted to move towards each other slowly. They both needed some assurance on the relationship, especially with Ronald still reeling from the pain of his failed first marriage. They even saw other people for a while. But by 1951, Nancy knew what she wanted and pursued it. With the possibility of moving away to New York for a role hovering over the couple's heads, Ronald finally popped the question.

"*Let's get married,*" he is reported to have said over dinner. "*Let's,*" was said to be her simple but profound reply. Just as simple was how they exchanged their vows, in a secret wedding on the 4th of March, 1952, at the Little Brown Church in California. At the time, Nancy was already pregnant with their eldest, Patti.

Later, Nancy Reagan would be quoted as saying that her life began when they met, but it was clear to many that the magnitude of their love went both ways. In letters to his wife (and there were plenty; *I Love You Ronnie*, published in 2000, is a book compiling their sweet correspondence from courtship to the White House), he would talk about how she was "*life itself to me*" and how she rescued him "*from a completely empty life.*" Even when they were married he would write, *"There would be no life without you nor would I want any."*

She still accepted acting roles after their marriage on film and television, but not very many. She would later write that her decision was due to witnessing the failure of many *"two-career Hollywood marriages."* The curtains would close on her professional life as an actress by the 1960s. She shifted to the role of full-time wife, homemaker and mother to Patti, born in 1952; Ron, born in 1958; and two of Ronald Reagan's children from his previous marriage to Jane Wyman, Maureen and Michael.

It wasn't all easy-sailing for the couple, especially when the Reagans had to struggle with Ronald's diminishing career and heavy financial obligations, including private school for the children, mortgages and the upkeep of a 320-acre ranch. But Ronald and Nancy's story of devotion and never-ending courtship would always be described as a great and historic one, not only for a President of the United States, but as a model of love and romance for everyone.

The letters are only one part of the proof. In speeches, she would be seen seemingly hanging on to his every word. They held hands openly and frequently. She was also one of the most involved FLOTUS ever to walk the White House, serving as Reagan's right-hand (wo)man, reportedly consulted by POTUS in many things. Her involvement would even land her the nicknames "Dragon Lady" and "Mrs. President."

Nancy's devotion and would extend even after he was diagnosed with Alzheimer's disease. She managed his schedule and was fiercely protective of his image – literally. She reportedly placed tight restrictions on what photographs that could be taken of the ailing former President.

Political Theater

Ronald Reagan may have been typecast as best friend or supporting character to the hero, and he might not have received wide recognition for his acting skills. But in the inner-workings of the Hollywood machine, he was the leading man in a larger story.

When he was a working actor, his intelligence, ambition and drive were clear to many, and this shone brightest in his dedication and involvement to the actors' union, the Screen Actors Guild ("SAG"). He had ideas, the courage to share them, the discipline to organize them, and the guts to pursue them even under pressure.

It may be recalled that he was a fresh face in the Hollywood scene in June, 1937. The SAG was on its early, shaky legs then, but Reagan was on board almost immediately, becoming part of the actors' union before the end of the month. Just a few years later, in 1941, he was already in the board of directors, where he would steadily climb to 3rd Vice President and eventually, President by 1947.

One of the improvements secured during his initial tenure (1947 to 1952) was residuals for TV actors; they would get some compensation for episode re-runs. Movie actors, however, would need to fight harder for the same right, if their films should be shown on television. Hollywood producers weren't quite inclined, but the actors and those negotiating on their behalf refused to let go of all the potential income. So they called upon Ronald Reagan's leadership and negotiating skills again. Part of the plan was the actor's strike on the 7th of March, 1960. Weeks later, a compromise was reached that was received well by most actors.

The effects of the deal landed by Reagan on behalf of his fellow actors continues to be felt to this day. Large residual payments reach actors both known and unknown, from media showing their work including television, cable, video and even streaming and downloads. There are also options for pension and health insurance.

Interestingly enough, these kinds of entitlements slant towards the Democratic and liberal, don't they? But why shouldn't they be – Ronald Reagan, Republican poster boy, started out as one. His parents were Democrats, his father and brother found work through New Deal programs, and

Reagan was a fan – not to mention a voter!- of Franklin D. Roosevelt. The Reagans had benefited from President Roosevelt's economic initiatives after all, but Reagan also identified with Roosevelt's sense of internationalism.

Defection and Scandal

Ronald Reagan's role in SAG was his first real taste of big-time politics with a large price tag. It was a microcosm of some of the conflicts and decisions he would have to face as the President of the United States. There were business interests versus pricey 'public' benefits, conflicting objectives, hard stances and hard heads, that he somehow had to bring all together to come up with a workable solution to keep the Hollywood engine running.

The benefits negotiated in his tenure on behalf of the union wasn't quite typical of the limited business intervention and small government mindset he would later espouse as a Republican. What could have accounted for the shift, especially since as recently as the 1950s, he was campaigning for Democratic candidates like Helen Gahagan Douglas, a liberal who had faced off and lost against Richard Nixon for a Senate seat? As Ronald Reagan would be famously quoted as saying, "*I didn't leave the Democratic Party. The party left me.*" What could he have experienced along the course of his life for him to decide that the Democratic Party no longer held true to his beliefs?

His marriage to nancy Davis and exposure to her conservative stepfather, Loyal, may have had a part in it. But also, in 1954, Ronald

Reagan started his stint as spokesman for General Electric. In this capacity, he was involved with hosting and acting for *General Electric Theater*, an anthology program that aired on CBS. The show was a success, running for eight seasons. It was actually pitched to GE's ad agency, BBDO so there was a tight branding and corporate messaging. For GE, part of that brand was science and progress. As a result, the Reagan family became a banner for a modern, electronic existence, and their home would embody it with advanced technology.

Aside from hosting and acting on television, Ronald Reagan also toured the country on behalf of General Electronic, as a spokesman / goodwill ambassador. Up to 12 weeks out of the year would be spent on the road, and at the end of his duties, Reagan had visited almost 140 facilities and faced over a quarter of a million of GE's workforce – live encounters he would have been sheltered from when he was just a performer in front of the camera on a soundstage. In his live appearances, Reagan showed not just his savvy communication skills but also a common touch and stamina, with as many as 14 speeches expected in a grueling day.

This was his political dress rehearsal, not only physically, but also in terms of helping to form his views of how a government should run.

Over the course of these tours, he spent many hours on the road with GE's PR man, Earl Dunckel, a self-described archconservative, with whom he debated and exchanged ideas. He was also exposed to antiregulatory views, via encounters with executives, managers and workers. His reading materials followed the same slant, including books like Henry Hazlitt's free-market classic, *Economics in One Lesson*. Slowly, his speeches began to be laced with messages of federal government shortcomings and overreach. He was starting to find government impositions as a threat to individual freedoms and a ceiling on individual achievements.

From a mix of influences and experience, as well as his own lively thinking, Reagan had started forging a belief system all on his own. From liberal he became more conservative. He was pro-business and against wasteful spending and too much government regulation. These aligned more with the Republican vision of government at the time than that of the Democrats'. He also began to fear his Party's seemingly increasing shift to the left. It did not help that the Democratic Party had internal struggles in the 1950s and the 1960s.

In 1952 and 1956, Reagan became part of Democrats-for-Eisenhower. By the next election though, he would be fully backing the Republican candidate Richard Nixon over the Democrats' golden boy, John F. Kennedy, and how – doing what was reportedly over 200 speeches for the Republican nominee. He continued to support Nixon, in the latter's (also) failed 1962 bid for California's governorship against Pat Brown, a Democrat. Reagan completed his conversion by changing parties in 1962.

Ronald Reagan was also dropped by General Electric that year. For a miscellany of reasons, it really was time for a change. But first, Ronald Reagan wouldn't escape Hollywood entirely unscathed.

In 1952, a SAG with Reagan at the helm granted his agent Lew Wasserman's MCA, a waiver that allowed them to become producers as well (there was a separate company set up for television production, Revue Productions). The ban stemmed from a SAG rule created to prevent conflicts of interest, if one entity became both an actor's employer as well as the agency negotiating for them. The waiver benefited not only Reagan's agency, which could now expand into the increasingly lucrative TV production field, but also himself; the General Electric gig he would get years later and keep for eight seasons became possible because of that waiver. The waiver issue would come back to haunt Reagan in 1962, when SAG and MCA became the subjects of an antitrust investigation.

SAG, through the waiver, may have given MCA the ultimate edge that eventually allowed it to become almost monopolistic, with control of a large percentage of the entertainment business. Ronald Reagan, as SAG President at the time the waiver was granted, was suddenly caught in the investigation. He testified before a federal grand jury in 1962, notably with incomplete recollections. His tax returns from 1952 to 1955 were also subpoenaed in a search for possible payoffs. No criminal charges were handed down from the investigation, but MCA would eventually sell of the agency arm to ease pressure exerted by the Justice Department. Some political analysts hypothesize that the scandal contributed to the loss of Reagan's GE job, but if it did, it would have been one of only a number of factors, including high costs, lower television ratings, and allegedly, Reagan's refusal to allow changes in the program's format. Either way, the incident just became more fodder for Reagan's growing view that federal government was stifling what he saw as legitimate business activities.

'A Rendezvous with Destiny…'

Reagan feared his Democratic Party was shifting too far leftwards for his taste. He had been exposed to views of the free market. He may have carried a grudge of his own against a government that forced itself into his private business affairs. His circumstances had also changed. He came from a family that benefited from FDR's New Deal programs, but now he was financially successful – with a tax obligation to match. All these may have contributed to Reagan's changed views on government.

Reagan, however, didn't just consolidate the main tenets of the political lens that would still hold a spell over our current Republicans, he was also unique in that he knew just how to package it. He was The Great Communicator. He understood people and knew how to talk to them. He was a good writer on top of being a gifted speaker with an affable, genial style and a quick, sparkling wit. He was also contagious in his notorious optimism. That gift for communication in politics wouldn't go unnoticed.

U.S. Senator Barry Goldwater of Arizona, co-author of *The Conscience of a Conservative* (1960), also had a yearning for less government intrusion and for his Party to be more a more distinct, conservative, alternative to the Democratic Party. He secured the Republican Party's presidential nomination for the 1964 elections, and tapped into the magic of Ronald Reagan. A week before the general elections, Reagan dazzled live and TV audiences with what would eventually be known as the "A Time for Choosing" speech, one of his seminal addresses in the sense that it not only espoused his core views, it also exposed his captivating style – "*You and I have a rendezvous with destiny.*" LBJ trounced

Goldwater in the general elections, but Reagan came out of 1964 as a beacon of light for conservatives.

The California governorship would be Reagan's first political test, both within his own Party and against the Democratic incumbent, Pat Brown. Brown, already a Republican 'killer,' seemed like a heavyweight compared to the actor. So the strategy by some supporters was to leak out information on Reagan's Republican rival, George Christopher to help Reagan secure the GOP nomination, then defat him in the general. Unfortunately for Brown, the move helped to unify the Republicans against him. They tried another tack; they packaged Reagan as an "extremist" right-winger, which had proven effective in discrediting Goldwater against LBJ in the general presidential elections. It wouldn't stick either. What could have stuck was Reagan's lack of experience, but the political newbie would overcome this hurdle by emphasizing the advantages of looking at things with a fresh perspective. It worked. Reagan would win over voters not only on his first run, but decisively. He would win his bid for re-election too, and served the state from 1967 to 1975.

His governorship of California is generally considered to be a successful one. His rhetoric stuck to conservative, but operationally, he was practical and willing to make compromises to achieve partial victories, even to the extent that he would work with liberals and democrats and at the cost of earning disapproval from his most conservative supporters. One might even look back at Reagan's accomplishments as a Governor and find them to be rather on the liberal side.

Consider, for example, that his time in office widened the sphere of legal abortion. Also, contrary to his campaign promises, the California government didn't get smaller, it got bigger. He did institute an early hiring freeze, but eventually Civil Service hires had to rise given an increase in demand for government service due to population changes. He raised taxes to balance the state budget (which was a constitutional mandate). His term saw an automatic cost-of-living increase on behalf of welfare mothers (versus his the antagonism his campaign expressed for 'welfare bums'). He was known to be pro-business and environmentalists were initially skeptical of him, but Reagan's time secured environmental protections for the state's north coast rivers, and blocked development that would have been detrimental to Lake Tahoe, the rivers Dos Rios and Eel, and the Sierra. His administration enlarged California's state park system by over 100,000 acres. He established boards for the control of water and air resources – which had an impact on car manufacturers improving their products' emissions and making cleaner cars. 20 percent of his first, top 100 appointments came from minorities, and California's first black head of a department was named by Reagan. He was harsher on the student unrests in California during his term though; "*obey the rules or get out*," he'd said, and was a hard-liner when it came to dealing with student violence, not fearing sending in the National Guard in dealing with them.

Still, he would leave his post as Governor of California with plenty of approval, Republican or grudging Democrat otherwise. And why shouldn't he? The financial scorecard he left with was impressive: $554 million budget surplus, and a triple-A state bond rating. And even when he was breaking the bad news or deviating from a promise, his charisma and self-deprecating humor carried him through.

The Road to the White House

'The B-movie Errol Flynn,' Ronald Reagan, was such a steady supporting presence on cinema, that upon hearing of Reagan's political ambitions, film mogul Jack Warner was rumored to have exclaimed, "*No. Jimmy*

Stewart for president, Ronald Reagan for best friend."

But Ronald Reagan, former SAG-President and by 1975, ex-Governor of the State of California, was about to play one of the biggest parts ever made on the world stage. He was a cool hand – staying in the public consciousness via speeches, radio recordings of commentaries, and a widely-read column that appeared in almost 200 newspapers nationwide.

Right around that time, one of the most significant events of American politics had just transpired. Republican President Richard Nixon left office in 1974 under the long, dark shadow of Watergate. He was succeeded by Gerald Ford, who picked liberal or moderate Republican Nelson

Rockefeller for his vice president – a move frowned upon by the conservatives. Rockefeller would be removed from the ticket come the 1976 elections, but Reagan's run was already in the cards; he was going to go against the incumbent Ford for the Republican presidential nomination. He lost by a slim margin, as establishment members of the Republican Party fell dutifully in line and backed Ford, who would eventually lose to the Democratic bet, Governor Jimmy Carter of Georgia. With Ford's defeat, Reagan looked to be next in line for his Party's nomination. The next elections were years away but he had his eye on the prize, and he was definitely in the game.

Ronald Reagan's Leading Role: President of the United States

Reagan declared his intentions to run in 1979, and would be going up against six other Republican hopefuls, among them Senator Howard Baker of Tennessee, Senator Robert Dole of Kansas, ex-Governor John Connally of Texas, Representatives Philip Crane of Illinois and John Anderson of Illinois, and former CIA director George H.W. Bush.

Bush presented a big challenge with the breadth of his experience within the Republican Party, the House, and internationally in China and the United

Nations. Bush had even won an upset in the first primary, and had belittled Reagan's economics as "*voodoo.*"

But with renewed vigor stemming from his surprise early setback, Reagan's inspiring communication skills and charm on the road, and a couple of stellar debate performances, Reagan won 29 of 33 primaries to cinch the Republican nomination. Ultimately, the race was really between him and Bush, who had won the balance. At the time, Reagan was the conservative standard bearer and Bush was the moderate choice – a conflict reconciled when Reagan picked Bush to be his VP running mate.

The Presidential Race of 1980 was on – between the Democratic bet, incumbent President Carter; the Republican nom,

Ronald Reagan; and moderate Republican, Representative John Anderson of Illinois. Anderson wasn't on board with Reagan's type of conservatism and ran as an independent, but he could still lure votes from moderates in the Republican Party away from Reagan. But Reagan wasn't the only one threatened by the third candidate; he had a liberal slant, and could bring in disaffected Democrats at a cost to Carter.

Early in the race, however, Reagan would be his own worst enemy. He had missteps from Mississippi to (in a sense) China, on highly contentious issues like state's rights and segregation, the Vietnam War, creationism, and support for Taiwan (versus established Sino-American relations). His views only served to feed the "extremist" image Carter's campaign was trying to foist on him – he could end up fracturing America, his hawkishness may send the country into another unwanted war, etc.. Unfortunately for Carter, he may have gone overboard in selling this image, which in excess, proved to be a disadvantage especially as Reagan began to rebound (aided in no small part by the big guns – his wife, Nancy, who knew how to manage his time and strengths), and focus on his advantage as a Washington outsider by attacking Carter's record. The candidates' respective temperaments also helped seal the deal; Reagan was sunny and optimistic, folksy, able to distill larger issues to common concerns. Carter, on the other hand, tended toward gloom and by his incumbent status, was forced to play on the defensive.

Reagan brought home this point during a debate set a week before the elections. "*Are you better off than you were four years ago?*" seemed a simple and straightforward question for the American voting public, and so were the ones that followed it, asking people about their experiences shopping, about unemployment, about America's standing in the world.

Come Election Day, they answered. And with a resounding 51% of the popular vote, and 489 electoral votes (versus 49 for Carter) in favor of Ronald Reagan, the 'Errol Flynn of the B's' was now the leading man of the world stage.

'Morning Again in America'

The domestic agenda was straightforward, with general themes that would be echoed by many Republicans to come after him: cut taxes, decrease government spending and balance the budget. By Reagan's rhetoric, big government was less of a solution to America's economic woes, and more of a hindrance to solving them. He laced his rhetoric with optimism, and sought to restore the country's confidence and sense of self – "*our capacity to perform great deeds*" as Americans. He also made good use of his pragmatic nature, and reached out to the Democrats who after all, held control of the House at the time. He also reached out to unexpected talent; he picked out James A. Baker III for chief-of staff in the White House, when Baker's previous experience included working with President Ford and George H.W. Bush when they were running against Reagan in 1976 and 1980.

It wasn't such an odd move for Reagan. When he ran for governor of California, he engaged the services of political consultants Stuart K. Spencer and Bill Roberts too, when they were previously working against Reagan's bet for the 1964 elections, Barry Goldwater. Appointments like these showed Reagan could be practical about surrounding himself with capable talent. He, after all, needed dependable men around him, due to a leadership style where he relied heavily on the delegation of day-to-day tasks. He, on the other hand, preferred to focus on the larger picture of dealing with Congress and pitching his fiscal policies. As a leader, he wasn't always the most knowledgeable offhand, but he did have a pulse on the American people, and was able to make and back tough decisions.

Unlike his recent presidential predecessors, Reagan was able to put immediate focus on the American economy. He wasn't saddled by Vietnam for example, and Iran had for whatever reason, released the American hostages they were holding during Carter's presidency when Reagan took his oath. But immediate focus did not necessarily mean success.

The basic pitch was to reduce tax and cut the budget. A tax reduction was viewed as an economic stimulus. The less taxes paid by corporations, for example, the more people they may hire. The more people who have jobs, the larger the tax base and the higher the demand for goods and services they now have money to spend on. The higher the tax base, the more the government revenue. The higher the demand for goods and services, the more production. With more production came more employment and more economic growth, and so on, and so on. It was based on a trust or belief in supply-side economics, and the trickle-down effect. As for budget cuts, the goal was to have a leaner government, and to set fewer regulations that restrict legitimate business activities. Eventually though, budget cuts turned out to be minimal. Though his rhetoric in setting 'bums to work' was harsh, Reagan could not really do anything to significantly alter safety nets like Social Security and Medicare, which were governed by formulas and laws that were especially difficult to challenge.

What ended up happening was almost a test of economic theory. A big tax cut and less revenues, while not having the corresponding decreases to spending, and as a matter of fact, including an increase in military spending, looked like a recipe for deficit and debt. Could the hope of supply-side economics for the trickle-down effect come through in this scenario?

But first, a more immediate problem: just a few months into the new President's term, a mentally-ill man named John Hinckley Jr. successfully put a bullet in his chest.

An appearance at a Washington, D.C. hotel ends in near-disaster when John Hinckley Jr. fired shots at Reagan's entourage as they were exiting, wounding a police officer, a Secret Service agent, and near-fatally, press secretary James Brady and the President himself. Brady would take a bullet to the head that would have permanent repercussions. The President escaped to within a literal inch of his life; the bullet missed his heart by around that breathtaking margin.

The irrepressible Gipper would win hearts all over America for his courageous response to the incident, with his wit and humor winning out. *"Honey, I forgot to duck,"* he famously said to his apprehensive wife. To the doctors operating on him, he managed to joke that he hoped they were Republicans.

Ronald Reagan was a gifted leader, but a bullet soon made him legendary.

Approval ratings spiked after the assassination attempt, not only among Republicans but also among independents and democrats. It was a boost to his legislative agenda – as well as to his re-election prospects. Shortly after the shooting? The tax cuts he'd been selling were given the green light. The near-death experience also impacted Reagan's sense of purpose. He began to see God-given responsibilities against nuclear war and toward peace. He reached out to the Soviet Union seeking dialogue. The shooting would also pave the way for the President to support some gun control – the Brady Bill, named for his wounded press secretary.

Come 1984, Reagan and Bush were the team to beat. It was no surprise that they would lock down the Party nomination. They were ending their first term on a high, with reduced inflation, lower tax rates, a decrease in unemployment, and a healthy GNP. There was a military build-up and a bold rhetoric to match, upping America's international stature.

Jimmy Carter's VP, Walter Mondale and his invigorating running mate, New York Congresswoman, Geraldine Ferraro, bore the Democratic challenge against them. But how to win against the popularity of Reagan? The answer, they would find, was – you can't. Mondale made an issue of the long-term detriments of Reagan's fiscal policy, but he promised to raise taxes to balance the budget and though responsible, who would honestly be enthused to vote for someone who guarantees that burden? He said Reagan was too old, but the witty incumbent would shoot this down with a hilarious one-liner that killed the issue completely: "*I am not going to exploit, for political purposes, my opponent's youth and inexperience.*" Even Mondale was laughing. Only a man of

Reagan's charms could skewer his opponent and leave them in stitches.

The final tally? 54 million votes to Mondale's 37 million, and an electoral college win for Reagan of 525 to 13. The old man carried all the states except for Minnesota (Mondale's) and DC. It's not just the overall numbers that count; Reagan proved winning to independents and a fifth of Democrats too.

The Iran-Contra Affair

Reagan's legend would be marred by a few inescapable issues.

In 1981, he signed an executive order authorizing secret CIA operations in support of the Contras, Nicaraguan rebels standing up against their country's leftist government. The secret backing wouldn't be secret for very long, and the House would respond to such activities with the Boland Amendment, which prevents American federal spending on attempts to overthrow the government of Nicaragua. Still, Marine Major Oliver L. North, part of the White House's National security Council, would have dealings with the Contras. He and a few of his cohorts would be able to find loopholes through which to aid the rebel group in arms supply. Elsewhere, Iran, Iraq's regional rival, sought to have discourse with the United States (who had for decades considered the government in Teheran as illicit, with the corresponding ban on arms sales to it). Soon though, a shipment of American weapons was made and shortly after that, an American hostage held by Islamic militants in Lebanon is released. In 1986, North makes a proposal: divert some of the proceeds from the Iran sale to the Contras.

Caught up in secrets was, apparently, what seemed like a deal of selling arms for hostages, and the illegal diversion of American federal funds in support of efforts to overthrow a foreign government.

The secrets soon unraveled and got mixed up in defenses and lies. By 1986, investigations were heavily underway, and links to top personalities in Reagan's White House were established. National Security adviser John M. Poindexter resigned; Colonel North was dismissed. Early the following year, special committees in the Senate and Congress were formed to get to the bottom of the issue, along with a Presidential commission. The latter commission announced the President wasn't involved in the NCS's operations; the Congressional Committees held the President to account for *"ultimate responsibility."*

The issue stretched into the early 1990s, and involved a litany of government personalities, including former National security adviser Robert C, Mcfarlane; former head of the CIA in Latin America, Alan D. Fiers; former chief of covert ops for the CIA, Clair E. George; former Assistant Secretary of Satte, Elliott L. Abrams; former chief of operations for the CIA, Duane R. Clarridge; former and Defense Secretary Caspar W. Weinberger.

The Iran-Contra Affair would also become one of the most glaring dents on the Reagan legacy. At the time, surveys showed low approval and trust ratings for the President. It wasn't only his trustworthiness that took a hit. If he didn't know about the intricacies of the secret deals and diversions, was he delegating too much? Was he too detached?

As Ronald Reagan was wont to, though, he managed a rebound. By the time he left office in 1989, his approval rating was the highest of any president since the legendary Franklin D. Roosevelt.

Exit Stage Left

Ronald Reagan clearly had his flaws. Some of his achievements were debatable too, especially those economic in nature and would acquire the catch-all term, Reaganomics – there were successes and duds, there were long-tern effects both good and bad that may or may not be attributed to them. His policies may have been right, right only for the particular context of his time, or wrong altogether in the larger picture. It is a mixed political legacy, as it usually goes for any man who held the office before him, and any man who would hold the office after him. It is the nature of the job, to not be able to please everyone, to never quite tie all the disparate threads together.

The Office of the President operates in a continuum of time. What may be right in the short term, becomes the next guy's problem (or the one after that or the one after that), later. It also does not operate in a vacuum; other factors play a part, including the other arms of government. A vision may not be enacted in its fullness – so why must it be judged as a failure in its objectives? The judgment of an American President, therefore, can have complex metrics.

In the case of Ronald Reagan, however, there were achievements that were squarely his own – the collection and articulation of a distinct and resonant vision of government that continues to captivate a large percentage of the American population. His intelligence and public appeal. His pragmatism and ability to work with politicians across the aisle. His quick wit.

His graceful exit.

In 1994, he penned a letter to the American people, revealing his Alzheimer's disease diagnosis. He used his prominence to bring awareness to a disease affecting millions of his countrymen. He also used the letter to express his love and gratitude to his country:

"...let me thank you, the American people for giving me the great honor of allowing me to serve... I will leave with the greatest love for this country of ours and eternal optimism for its future... I know that for America there will always be a bright dawn ahead."

However one thinks of Reagan, he was and continues to be a political force we would have to reckon with for years to come. He was transformational and inspirational; even in his exit, in the announcement of the disease that would eventually claim his life, he was a patriot and an optimist.

Made in the USA
Coppell, TX
08 January 2020